TANA HOBAN

I Walk and Read

Greenwillow
Books
New York

for my
brother
Russell

Library of Congress
Cataloging in Publication Data

Hoban, Tana.
I walk and read.
Summary: Color photographs
introduce signs seen
on streets.
1. Signs and signboards
—Juvenile literature.
[1. Signs and signboards
—Pictorial works]
I. Title.
HF5841.H57 1984
001.55′2   83-14215
ISBN 0-688-02575-7
ISBN 0-688-02576-5 (lib. bdg.)

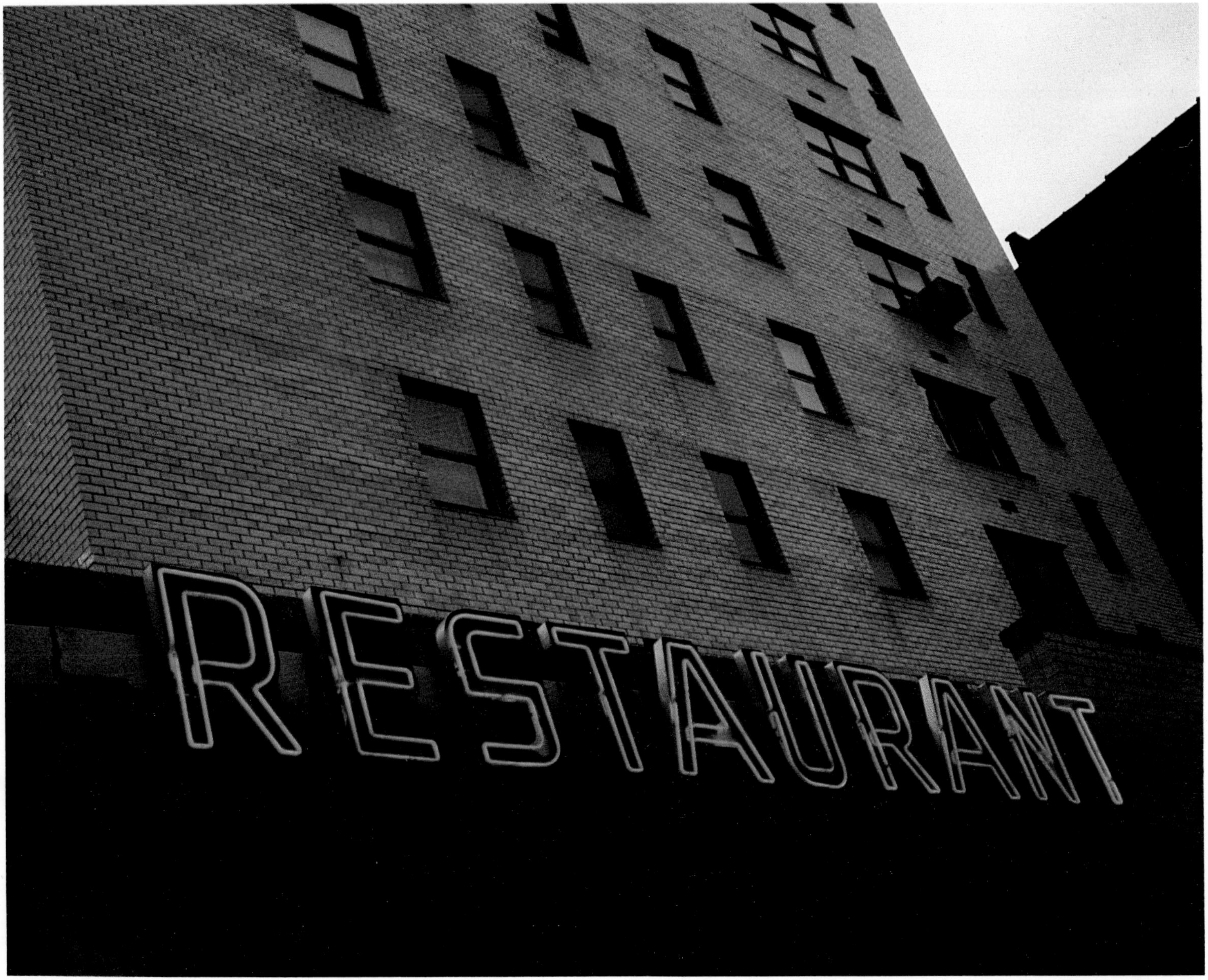
RESTAURANT

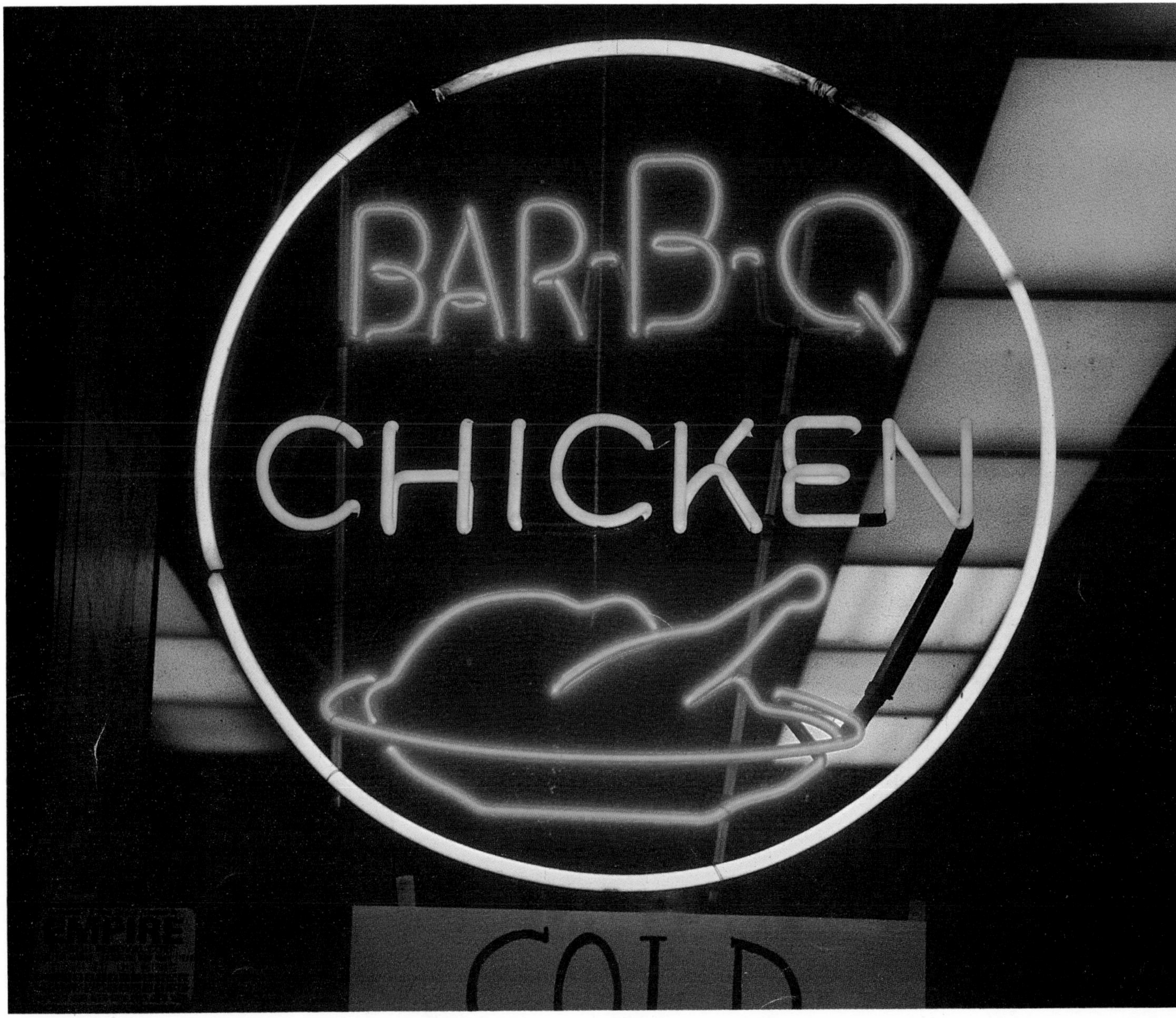
BAR-B-Q
CHICKEN

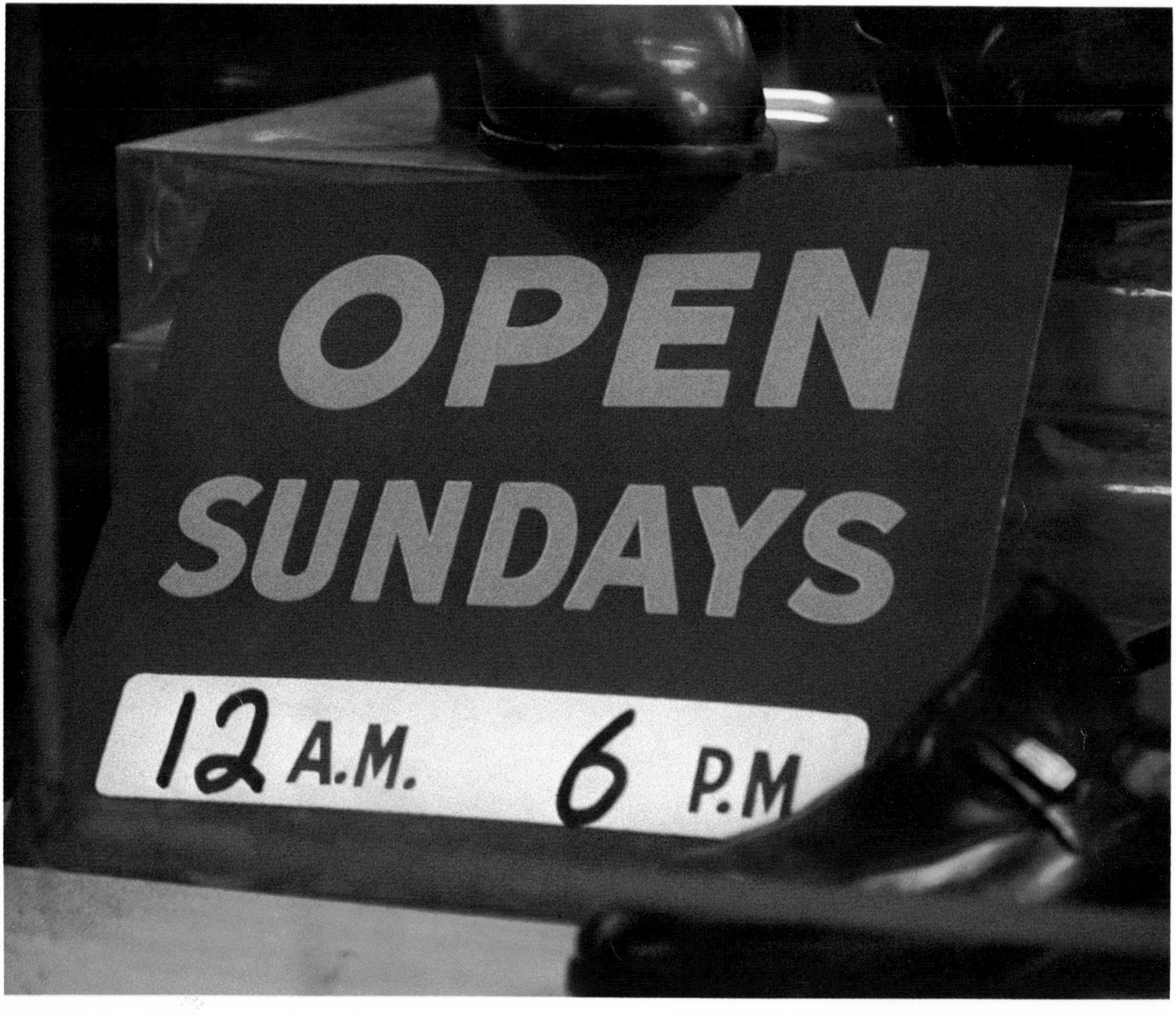
OPEN
SUNDAYS
12 A.M. 6 P.M

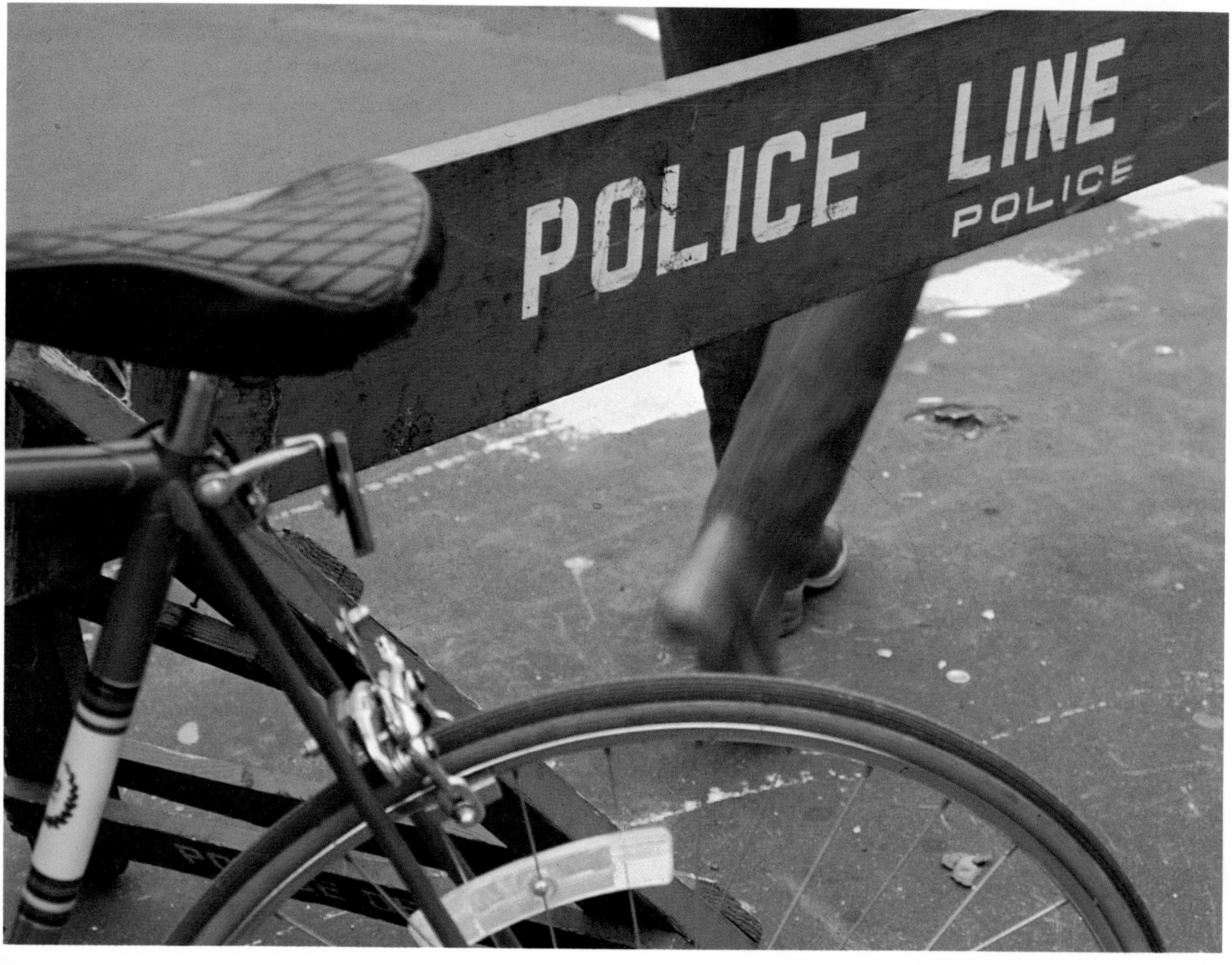
POLICE LINE
POLICE

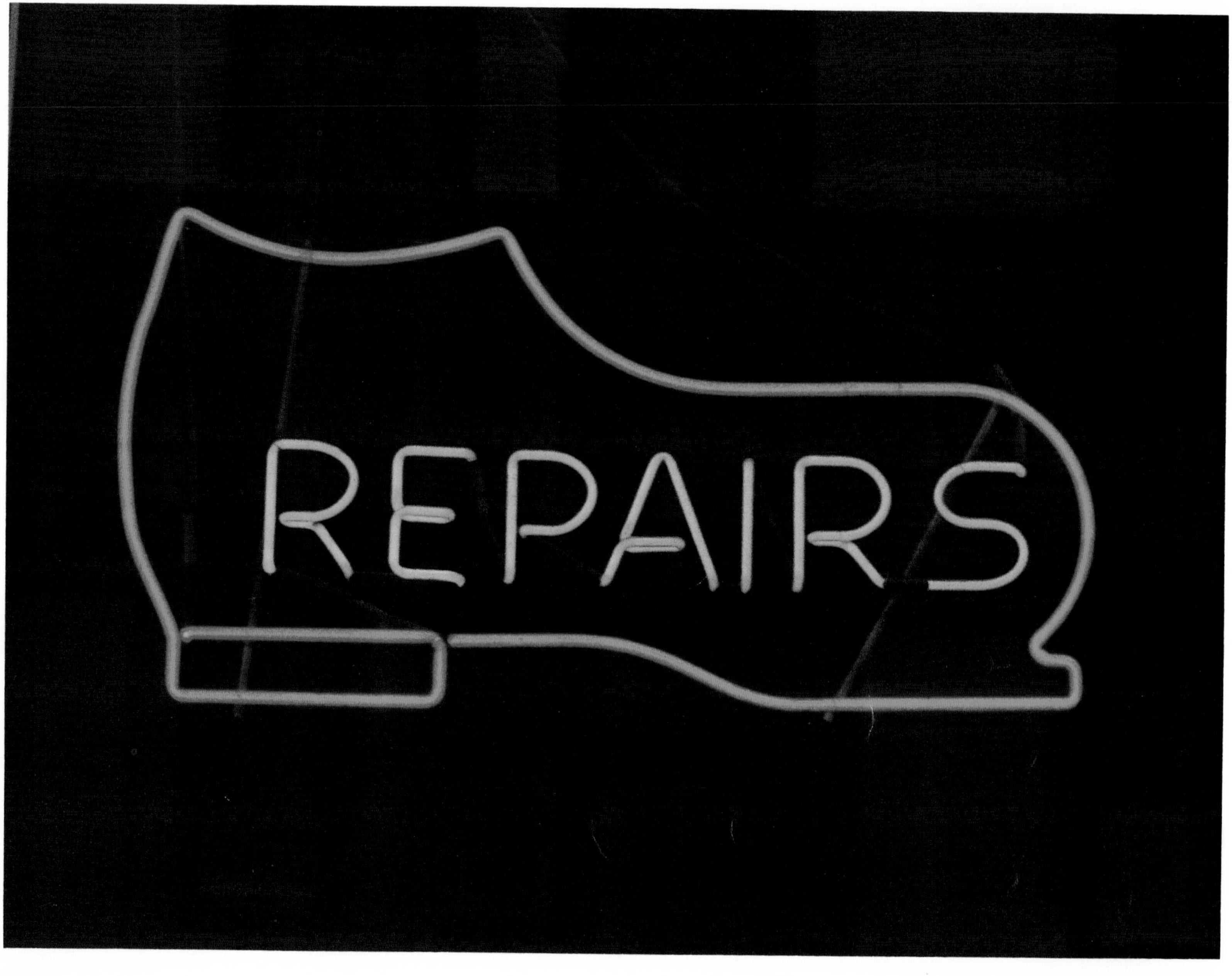
REPAIRS

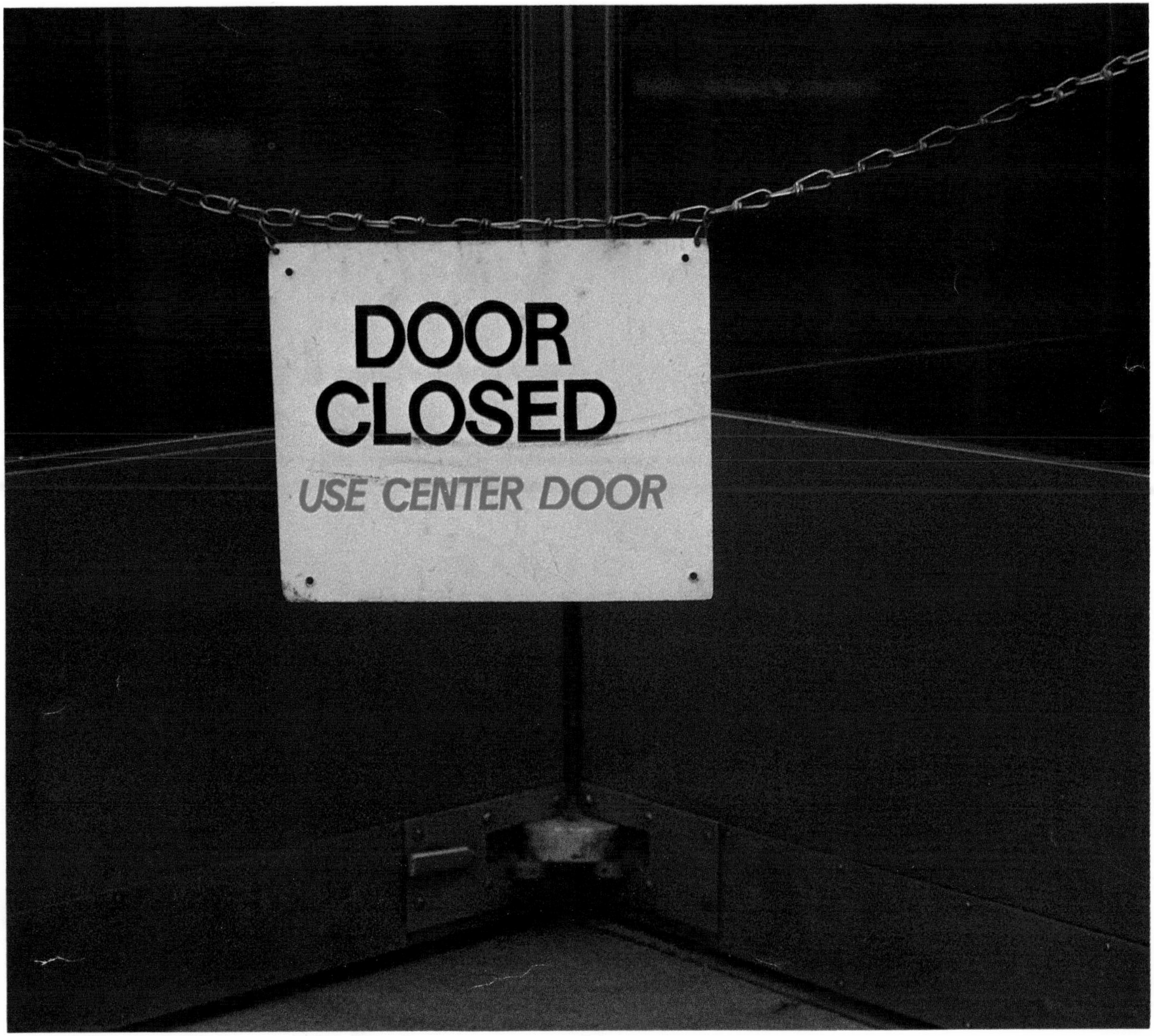
DOOR
CLOSED
USE CENTER DOOR

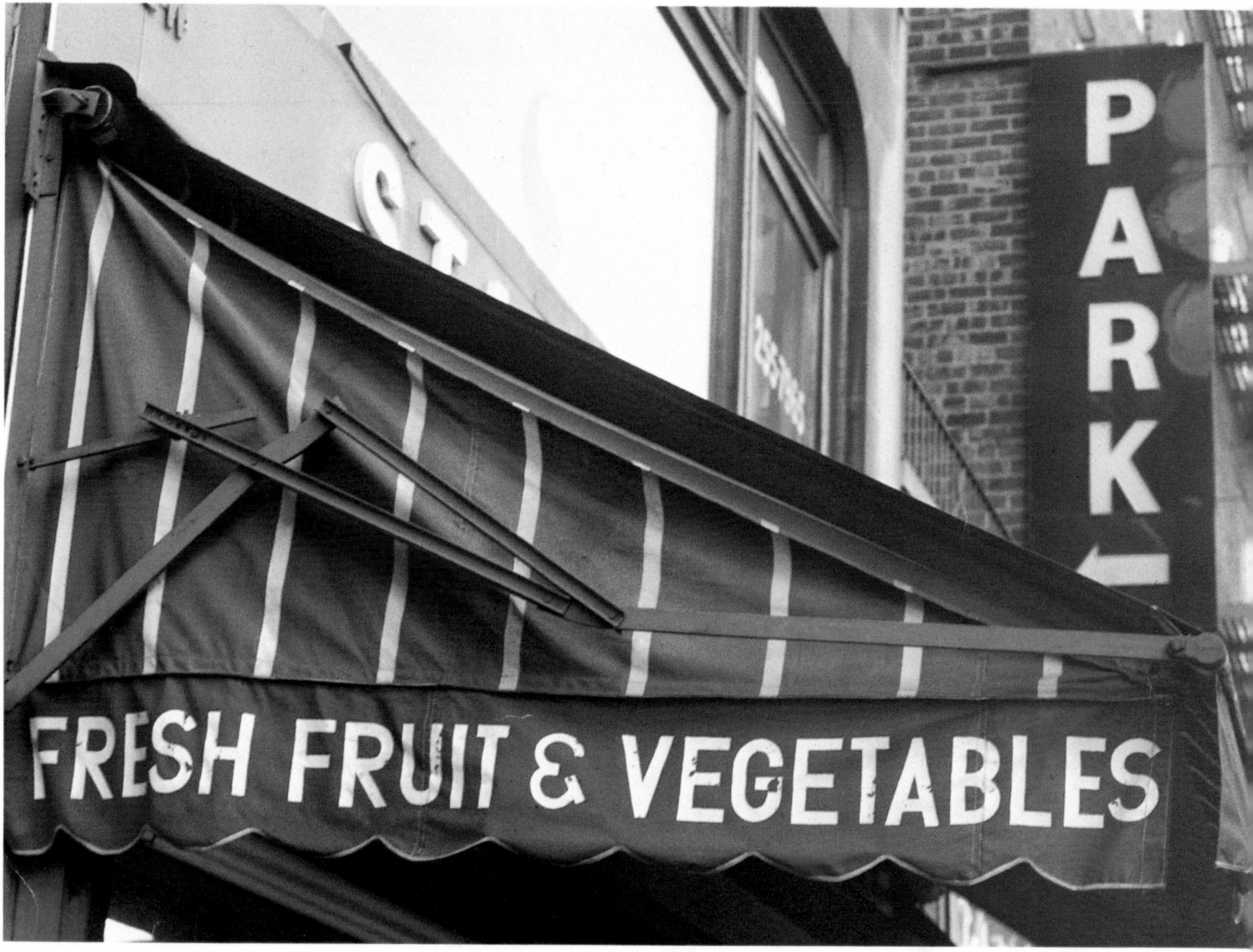
FRESH FRUIT & VEGETABLES
PARK

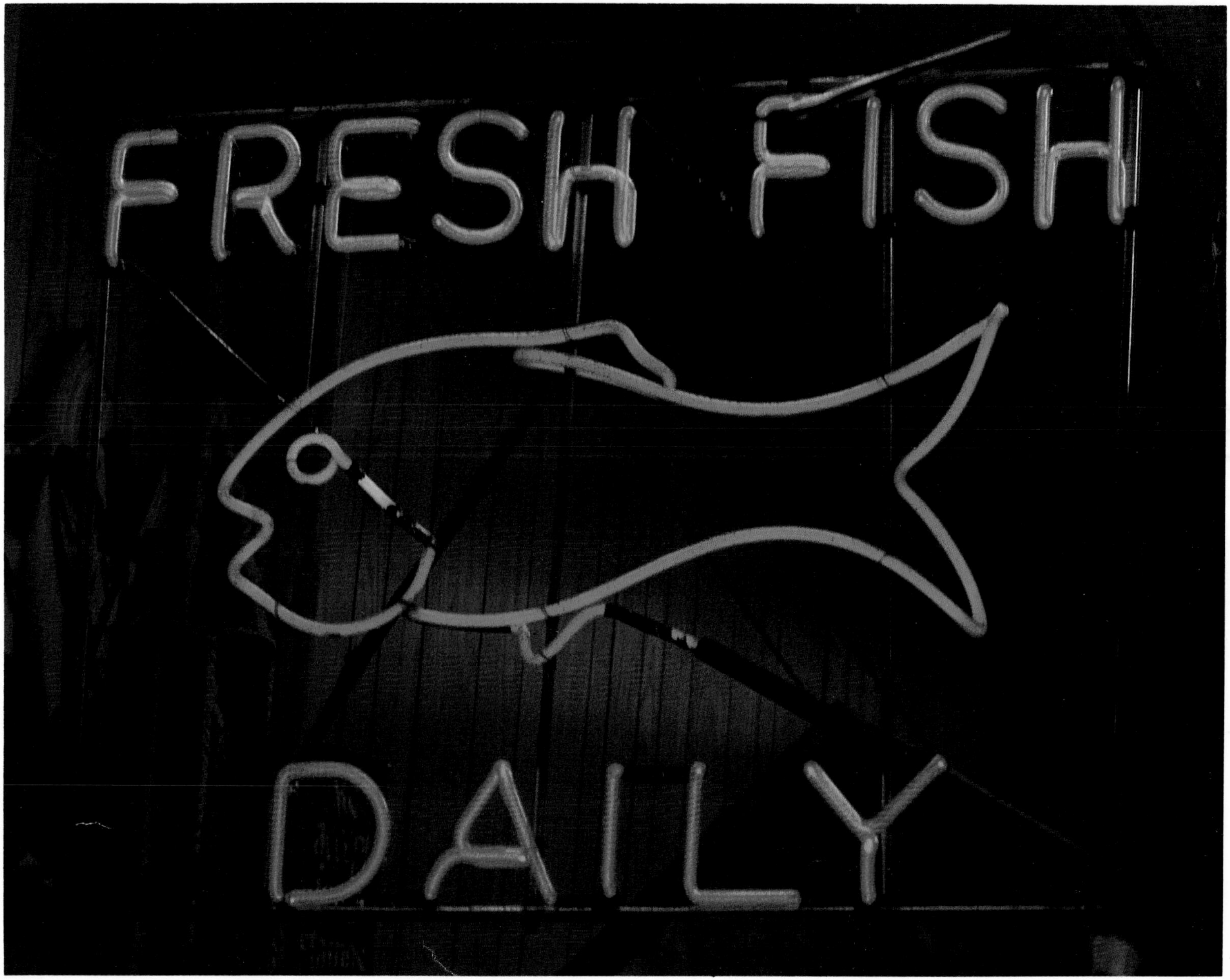
FRESH FISH
DAILY

14 · ENGINE · 14

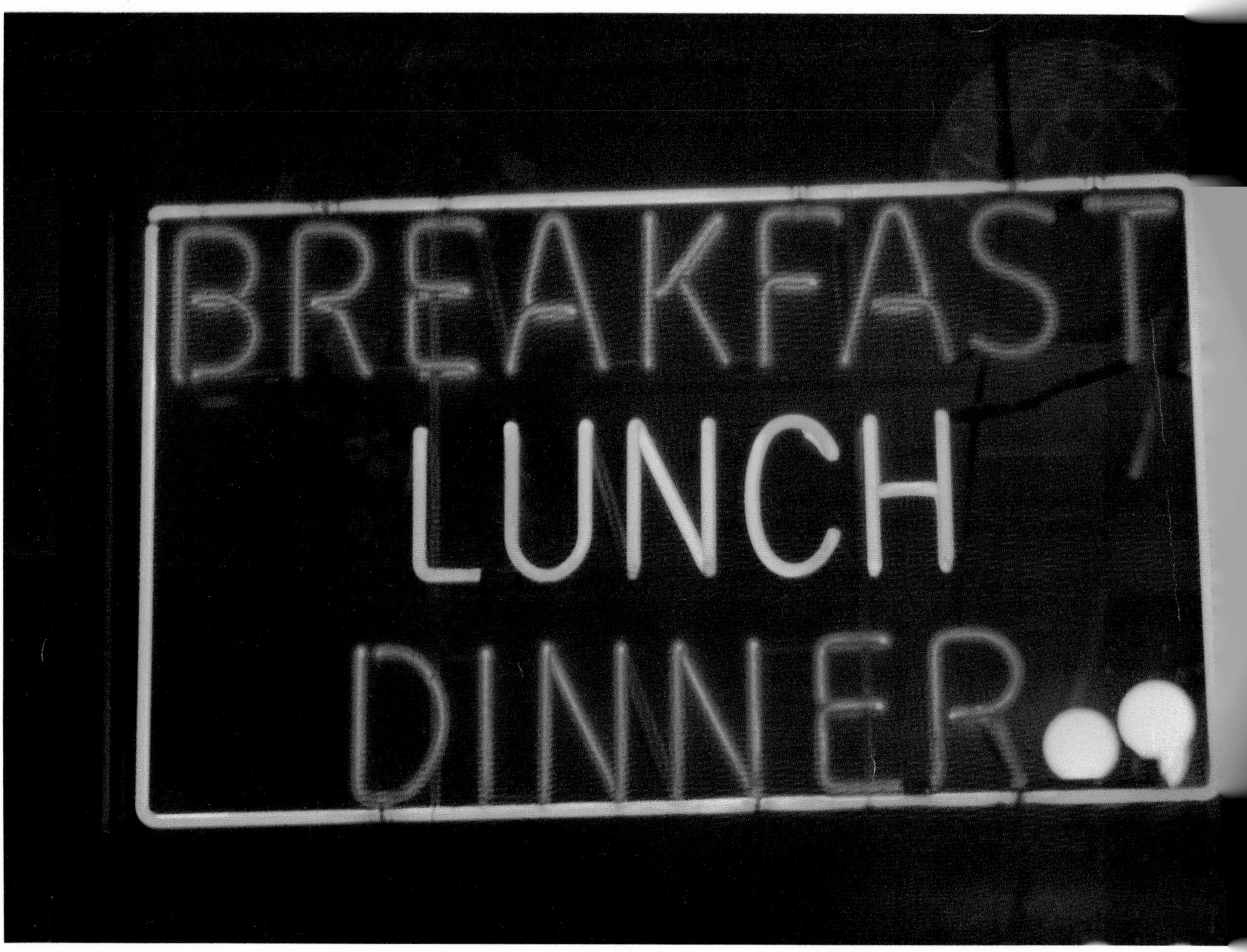
BREAKFAST
LUNCH
DINNER

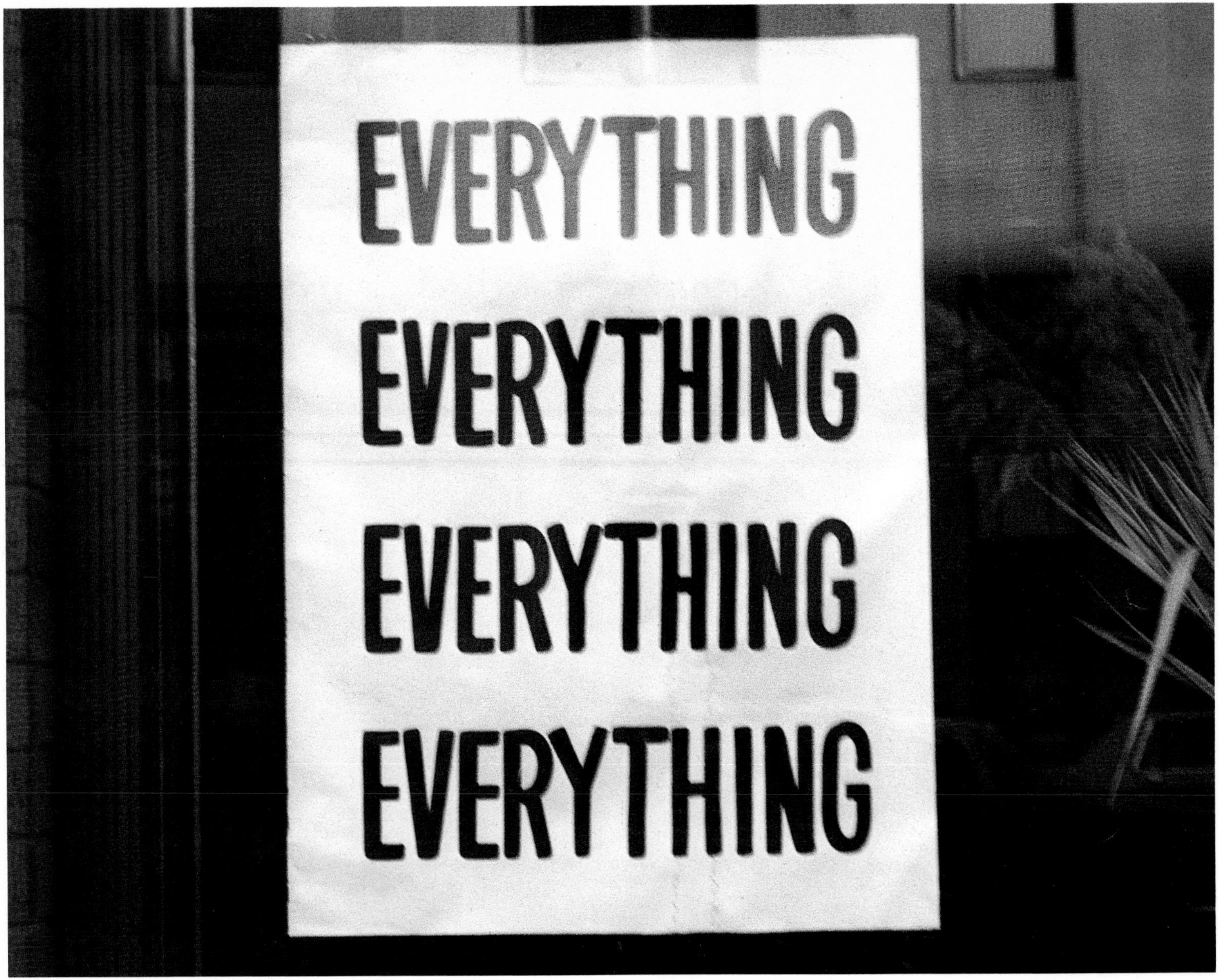
EVERYTHING
EVERYTHING
EVERYTHING
EVERYTHING

Museum Entrance ↑

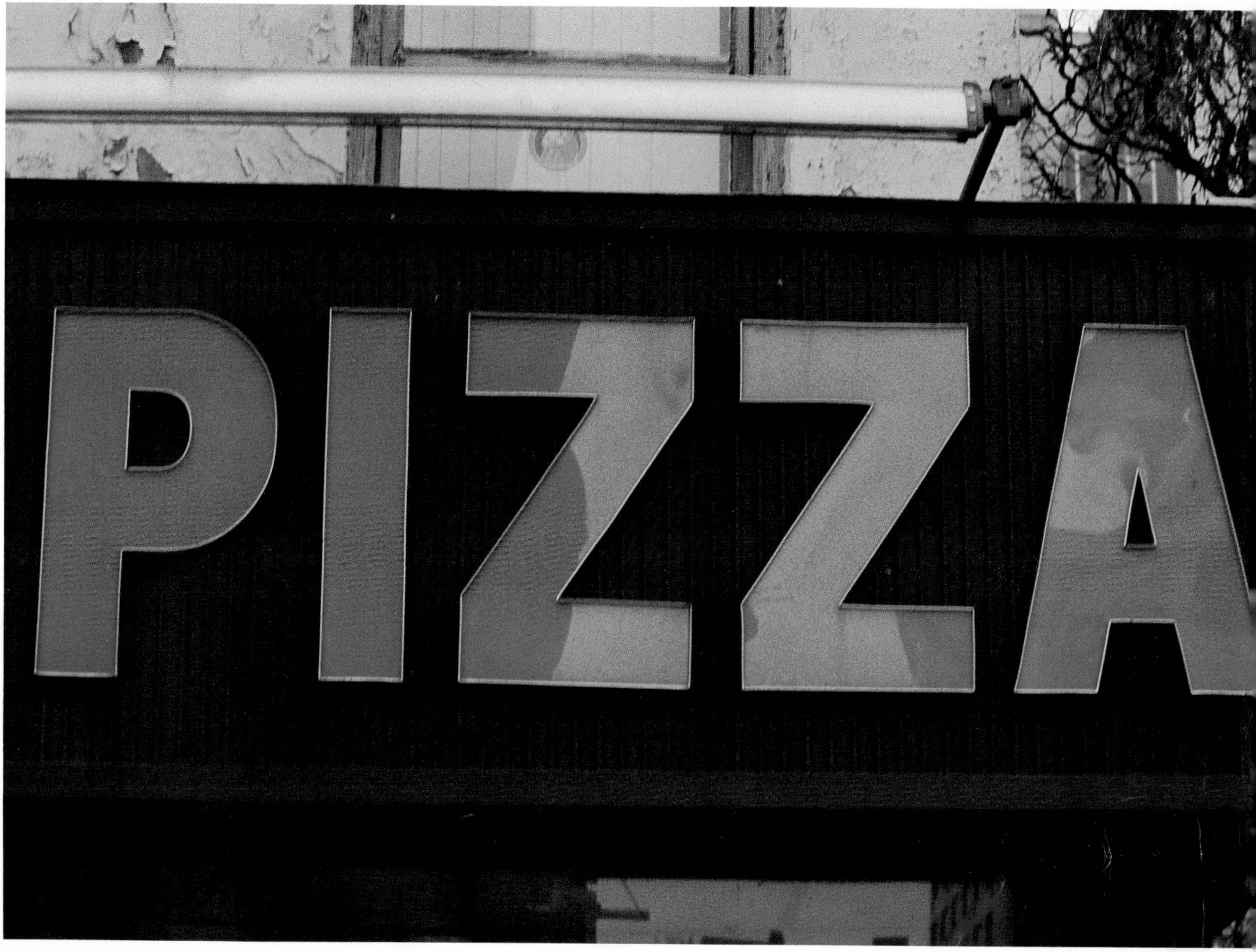
PIZZA

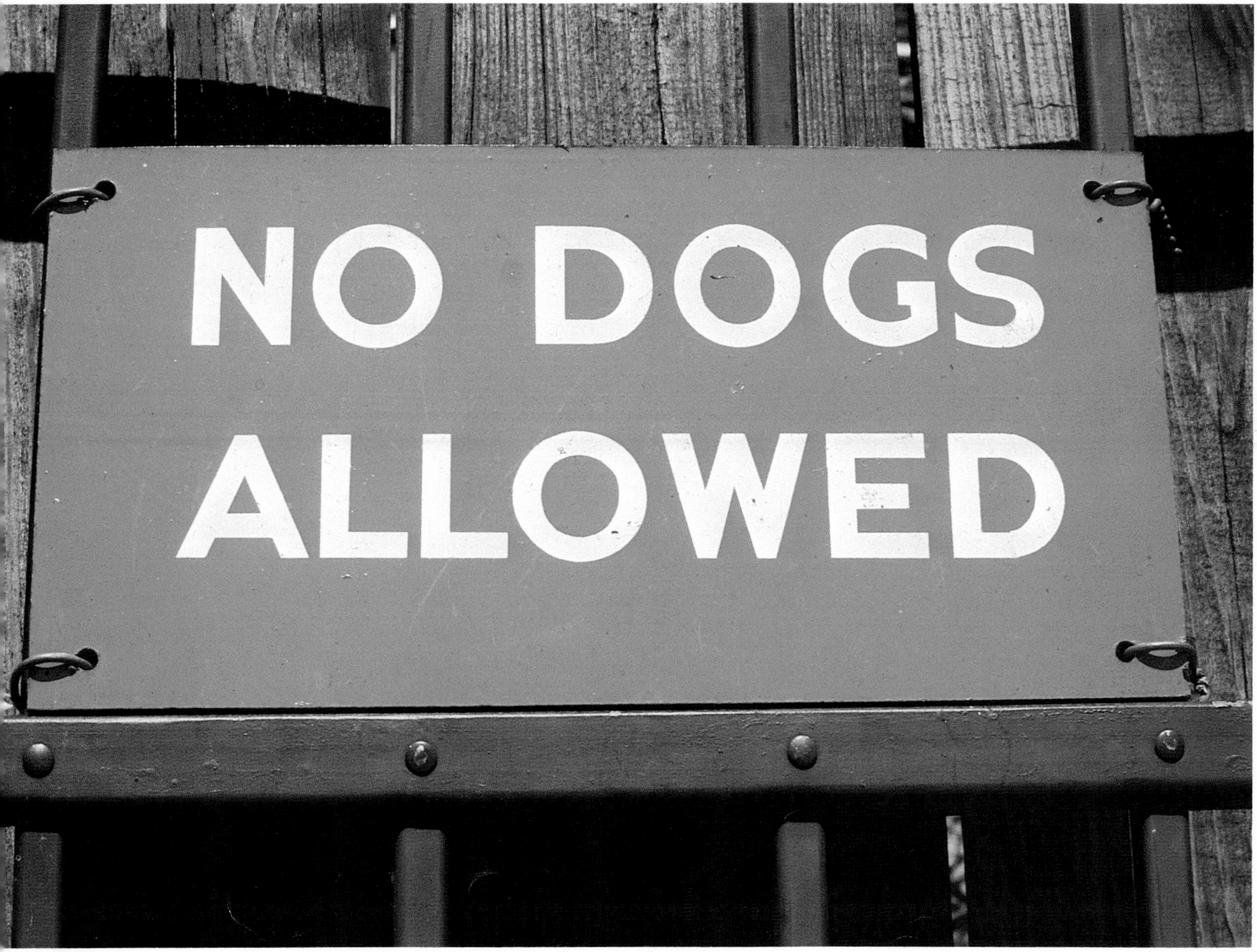
NO DOGS
ALLOWED

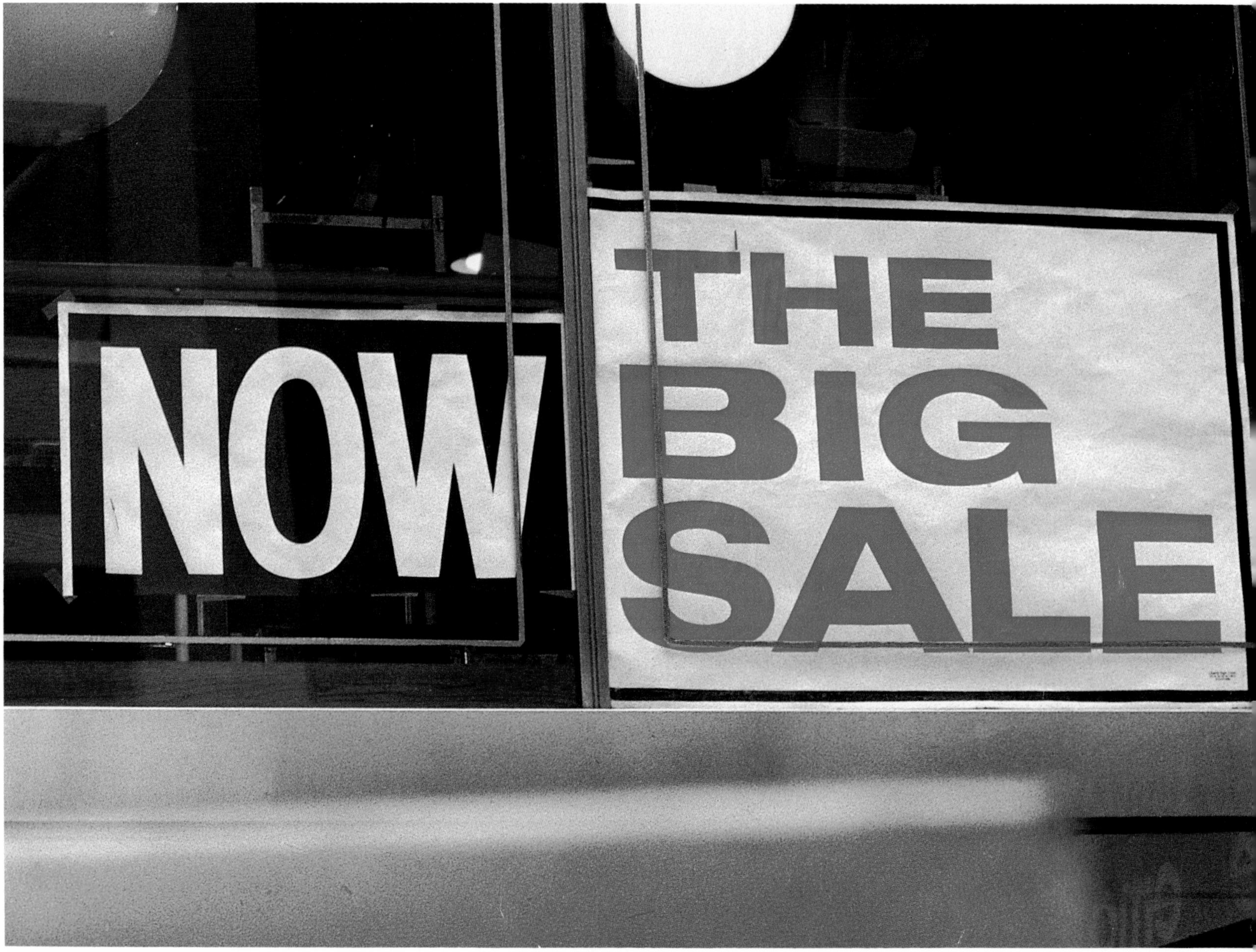
NOW
THE
BIG
SALE

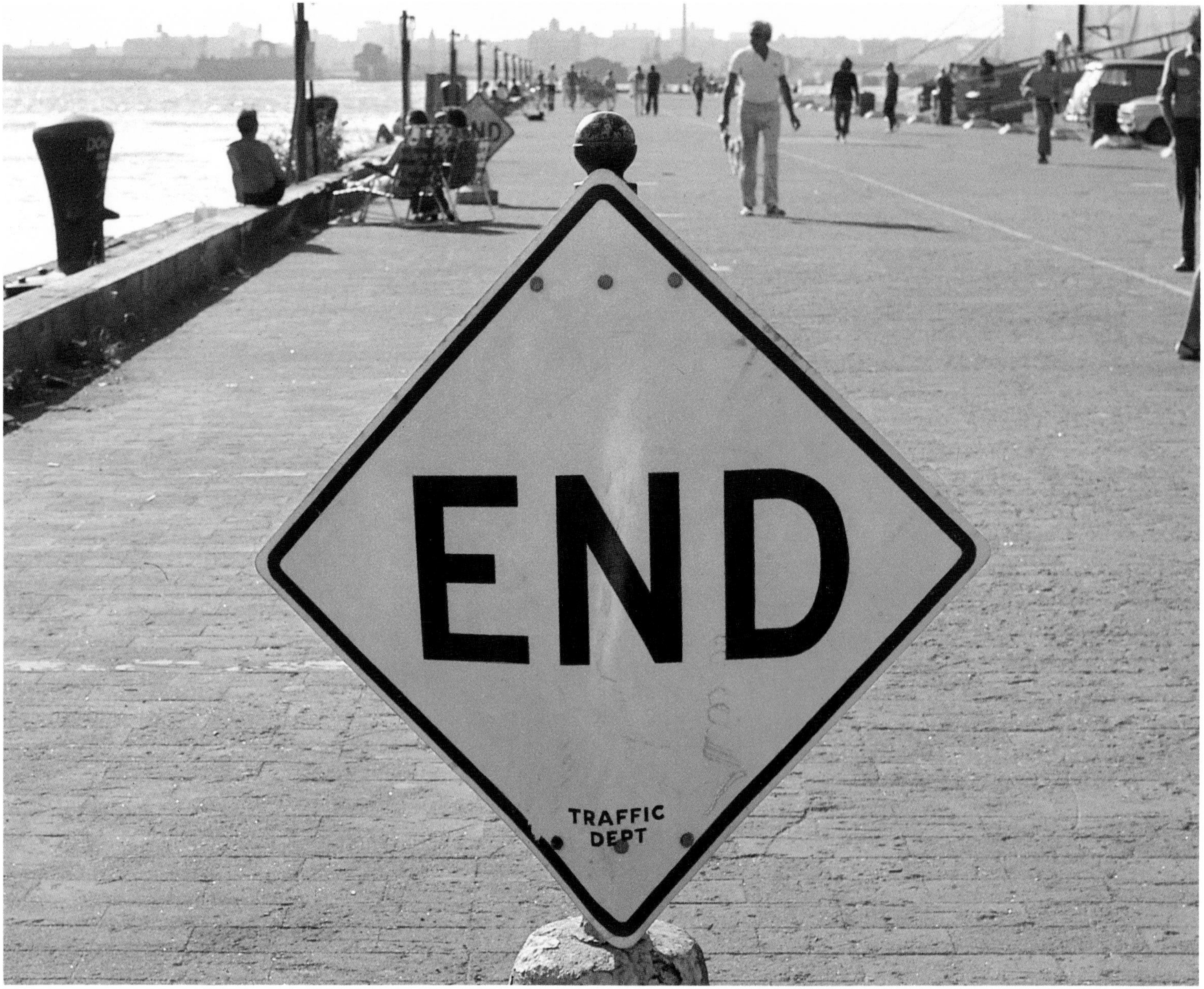
END
TRAFFIC
DEPT